To Dad

Committed to This Awesome Calling

TIM WESEMANN

Beacon Hill Press of Kansas City
Kansas City, Missouri

Copyright 2002
by Beacon Hill Press of Kansas City

ISBN 083-411-9501

Printed in the
United States of America

Cover Design: Michael Walsh

All Scripture quotations are from the *Holy Bible, New International Version*® (NIV®). Copyright © 1973, 1978, 1984 by International Bible Society. Used by permission of Zondervan Publishing House. All rights reserved.

Library of Congress Cataloging-in-Publication Data

Wesemann, Tim, 1960-
    Dad to dad : committed to this awesome calling /
Tim Wesemann.
      p. cm.
    ISBN 0-8341-1950-1 (pbk.)
    1. Fathers—Religious life. 2. Fatherhood—Religious aspects—
Christianity. I. Title.

BV4846 .W47 2002
242'.6421—dc21

                                                  2001043868

10   9   8   7   6   5   4   3   2   1

Contents

1. Wrapped Around Her Little Finger   5
2. Have Me Committed   9
3. A Father's Tribute   13
4. A Family Psalm   17
5. ABC's for Dads   21
6. Giving a Lift   25
7. All I Need . . .   29
8. The Best Ever   33
9. Bedside Thoughts   37

1
Wrapped Around Her Little Finger

Isa. 53:4-5

First a thud. Then a cry . . . more like a wail. I went running. It was serious, because the crying and the tears were coming from a little girl, and I was her daddy. It's *always* serious when that's the scenario! As far as the damage, it was just a scraped knee—not so serious.

My wife and I tried all the boo-boo distraction tactics we knew. We called for her boo-boo bunny. We tried crying with her. We held her tight and sang feel-good songs in her ears. These all seemed to make it worse. What was left? A bandage?

"Yyyeeesss!" came the reply.

Could it really be that simple? I grabbed one with her favorite cartoon character on it. We started to place it over her scraped knee, when Sarah let out another scream: "Nooooo!"

"But I thought you wanted a bandage."

"I . . . [sniffle, sniffle] *do!*" With that she held out the index finger on her right hand.

"But sweetheart, you hurt your *knee,* not your finger."

"WWWhhhaaa!"

She won. The bandage was swiftly wrapped around her little finger, and immediately the crying stopped (exception of those funny little postcrying gasps that have no name). She wiped the tears from her eyes onto her sleeve, and everything was fine.

To this day I'm not sure I'll ever understand that one. I'm thinking of having this case written up in the Harvard Journal of Boo-Boos!

Little Sarah was miraculously satisfied when the bandage was wrapped around her finger, while her knee was left uncovered with a trickle of blood running down her leg. With that substitutionary act, life was full, happy, and back to normal.

I scratched my head as Sarah walked away while God scratched at the door of my heart. He reminded me of all *my* boo-boos—

"sin" is the word He used. He reminded me of my tears. He reminded me of times I tried to justify my sins, hide them, and forget them. It didn't work. My sins were against God, but through them I had also hurt others. The sins occurred in every aspect of my life, and yet Jesus took me somewhere else. He led me to a hill outside Jerusalem, where we stood in the shadow of a Cross. There He bandaged up all my sins and wrapped His healing words around my heart and hurts.

He said, "Surely, I took up your infirmities and carried your sorrows. . . . I was pierced for your transgressions, I was crushed for your iniquities; the punishment that brought you peace was upon Me, and by My wounds you are healed" (Isa. 53:4-5, author's paraphrase).

He won! The bandage of forgiveness was swiftly wrapped around my life, and immediately my sins and their scars were removed and forgotten. He wiped my tears with His blood-stained sleeve. All that remained were those little postforgiveness gasps of thankfulness.

To this day I'm not sure I'll ever fully understand grace like that. But it's been written up in the Book of Life, and so I believe. With His substitutionary act, my life is now full and happy. I walk forgiven while blood flows from His life-giving body hanging on the Cross.

Little Sarah may have me (and a bandage) wrapped around her little finger. But it's more important that Jesus has wrapped His cross around our lives as He forgives us, holds us, wipes our tears, and makes everything fine.

FATHER TO FATHER: *I may not ever fully understand Your grace, but I accept it, rejoice in it, and respond to it by giving You my life. In Jesus' name I pray. Amen.*

2
Have Me Committed

Matt. 6:33

Fatherhood is an awesome calling. Much of what we do with our calling as fathers will affect our children all through their lives.

Consider how your father affected your life. Does the way he communicated with your mother affect the way you now communicate? The same goes for how he dealt with frustration and anger. How often do you hear words coming out of your mouth that uncannily resemble your dad's words? How has your dad's faith, or lack of it, affected yours? Have you felt the effects of his love in the way you love? Compare your work ethic to your father's. How influential has your dad's presence, or lack of presence, in your life been as you're now called to be a father? What physical attributes, emotional capabilities, or spiritual traits do you share with your dad?

Most often we are who we are because of what we learned in our homes. We're comfortable with what we know, and we continue in those ways. There are also times when the Lord takes negative childhood experiences and uses them positively when we're adults.

The powerful effect—positive or negative—that our fathers have had on us is amazing. And now *we* are fathers who are affecting *our* children's lives. What an awesome responsibility!

We need to stand in awe of this calling and ministry. Fatherhood calls for a great commitment from people who live in a world that seems to know little about that subject. Being a father takes energy and work, as do all of our relationships—and it will have a lifetime effect on our children.

Overwhelmed? Discouraged? Feel inadequate for the task? If so, know that help not only is on the way but has arrived! Our Heavenly Father points us to His Son, with whom He is one. We are called into His presence for encouragement and help for the joyful task at hand. He promises to walk with us through it all. He promised that when we commit our ways to Him, He will pour out

His blessings. As we seek His kingdom first, He will place the riches of heaven at our feet.

He also calls us to find our adequacy in Christ. When we rely on our own strength in this monumental calling, we'll find sin, failure, and inadequacy. We must keep our lives aligned with His and esteem Him for who He is. Then we find Him lifting us higher than we've ever been before.

He promises forgiveness to His repentant people—fathers included! With that gift, the opportunity is there to right any wrongs we may have created in the lives of our children. He is the God of reconciliation. He is the healing God of scarred relationships. He is God. That says it all.

Setting Him apart as Lord in our hearts means He will bring out His best in us. When that occurs, we will have a God-pleasing, eternal effect on our children. What a joy to go into fatherhood eternally affected by our Father and His gifts of forgiveness, grace, and power!

FATHER TO FATHER: *Fatherhood is an awesome calling. You are an awesome God. I commit all that I am and have to You. In the name of Jesus I come. Amen.*

3
A Father's Tribute
1 Cor. 1:18-24

A white cross looms over the city of Acapulco, Mexico, against a backdrop of the blue Mexican sky. It juts out of the top of a mountain and can be seen from most spots of the city and its beautiful bays. At night a cascade of lights illuminates it. During the day the bright sun reflects off the white paint, keeping it a focus point for residents and tourists. Sitting in the shadow of the cross is a church building.

This cross is more than an imposing structure on the hilly landscape. A father constructed it as a memorial for his two sons who died in a 1967 airplane crash. The father has an ever-present, powerful reminder of his sons' death. As long as he is near the city, the cross will always be visible and the memory fresh. When the father and his family see the cross, I wonder: do they remember primarily the tragic way these young men died, or the way they lived? Regardless, the death of his sons will not be forgotten.

The father could have constructed a statue of his sons. He could have built a memorial in the shape of the airplane in which they died. But he chose a cross, like that on which the Savior of the world died, which serves as a constant reminder of His death. It is an *empty* cross—symbolizing the resurrected, living Savior. The lights that surround it break through the darkest hours. The cross rises against the backdrop of the heavens. It is seen by all, and at its base is a church where the gospel of Jesus Christ is proclaimed. What a great memorial indeed! It is the memory of the love of two fathers—the love of an earthly father and the love of a Heavenly Father—which made living possible even amid death.

I would imagine that people who live near the cross in Acapulco get so used to it that they don't pay much attention to it. Unfortunately, that can also be true for those of us who live beneath Calvary's cross. It's tempting to take its grace-filled message for granted. We could easily walk by it week after week without being affected by its awesome message. Satan would love for us to see it as more of an eyesore and hindrance than the message of hope, forgiveness, and eternal life that it is.

Maybe that's why the father built the cross so large. Was he hoping he would never forget, never take for granted, never fail to be affected by *the* Cross? May that be our prayer.

As I looked at that particular illuminated cross one dark evening, the last verse of the hymn "Abide with Me" ran through my mind:

Hold Thou Thy cross before my closing eyes;
Shine thro' the gloom, and point me to the skies.
Heav'n's morning breaks, and earth's vain shadows flee.
In life, in death, O Lord, abide with me.

—Henry F. Lyte

I don't know the father whose sons died in a plane crash. But I'm glad that both of us know a Father whose Son died on a cross on a hill called Calvary. What a powerful, constant memorial of life for us to keep our eyes on at all times!

FATHER TO FATHER: *Father, hold Your Son's cross always before me and my family. Illuminate it so its message might reflect off us. In life, in death, O Lord, abide with us. In the name and living memory of Christ crucified I pray. Amen.*

4
A Family Psalm
Ps. 136

Ps. 136 is a prayer of praise to God that celebrates His eternal love and reminds us of His incredible grace. It is thanksgiving-inspired and gives a word of encouragement for the future. The psalm is repetitive: 26 times it proclaims the phrase "His love endures forever." The psalmist gives thanks to the Lord and reviews His mighty acts from creation to the entrance into the Promised Land. It is a psalm for the family of God, about God and His family. So is this:

Give thanks to the Lord, for He is good! *His love endures forever!*

Give thanks to the Lord of lords and Lord of our family. *His love endures forever!*

To Him who knew us before we were a family. *His love endures forever!*

Who created the world and our faith through His Word. *His love endures forever!*

Who breathed into us the breath of life, filling our lungs with air and our hearts with an eternal hope. *His love endures forever!*

To Him who allowed our children to take first steps and the Spirit-created ability to follow in His steps. *His love endures forever!*

To Him who created smiles for us to wear, along with an unseen sign of the Cross that marks us as ones redeemed by Christ the crucified. *His love endures forever!*

To Him who gives us shelter and food while covering us with His love as we drink from His living water. *His love endures forever!*

To Him who carried us through thousands of diapers and hundreds of childhood stages. *His love endures forever!*

Through first words, school tests, lost teeth, and lasting memories. *His love endures forever!*

To Him who carried us through weeks of chicken pox and has healed our diseases. *His love endures forever!*

To Him who compassionately led us through times of darkness and family deaths directly into the eternal promises of life. *His love endures forever!*

To Him who graciously entrusts us with more than we need and more than we ask for. *His love endures forever!*

To Him who gives us reason to focus on what lies ahead. *His love endures forever!*

As we focus on the message of His cross, which leads us home. *His love endures forever!*

Walking together, hand and heart in His. *His love endures forever!*

We walk with confidence and joy as a family within His family. *His love endures forever!*

To Him who gave His life for this family and all families, be all praise, honor, and thanksgiving. *His love endures forever!*

Give thanks to the Lord, for He is good! *His love endures forever!*

FATHER TO FATHER: *Father, Your love for our family endures forever. May our love for You also endure forever. All praise, honor, and thanksgiving be Yours! In Your Son's name we pray. Amen.*

5
ABC's for Dads
Rev. 1:8

Jesus referred to the first and last letter of the Greek alphabet when describing who He is and what He is about. He is the First and the Last, the Alpha and the Omega, and everything in between. We should strive to be all that He would want us to be as fathers. With that in mind, here are some ABC's for dads.

A—ccepting your children as they are encourages them to be all the Lord wants them to be.

B—ible. Base your parenting, marriage, job, relationships, thoughts, and daily life on God's Word.

C—ompassion is not a sign of weakness, but one of great strength in the Lord, whose heart goes out to you.

D—iscipline in love is a necessary tool for a father who loves his children.

E—xample. Your actions and words have a powerful, lasting effect on your children. Pattern your life after the Lord's as your children stay within the pattern you leave them.

"**F**—orgiven and forgiving" is your story through Christ's gifts. Pass the gifts on.

G—od-fearing. Stand in awe of the ultimate Father as you father.

H—ope with a sure certainty of God's promises while you walk daily as both a parent and as His dearly loved child.

I—nterest in your children's interests says to them, "I love you!"

J—oke around more! Lighten up!

K—now your family—their needs, wants, joys, fears, likes, and dislikes.

L—ove. Nothing more needs to be said.

M—om-lover. Love your children's mother.

"**N**—o." It's a necessary word at times, but not at all times.

O—asis. Create a godly home for your children that's an oasis in the midst of their wilderness days.

P—lay!

Q—uake in God's presence. You are on holy ground.

R—ejoice! I will say it again: *Rejoice!*

S—ervant father. You are called to a position of authority. You are also called to serve.

T—hankfulness. Give thanks, father, for the showers of God's blessings.

U—ndermine the plans that Satan has to undermine your family.

V—erify the love you have for your family daily in words and actions.

W—orship the Lord faithfully and joyfully with your family.

X—(Sometimes there are no words to describe the calling to be a godly father!)

Y—earn to follow closer in the Father's footsteps.

Z—est. Add this to your personal prayer list and to your life.

FATHER TO FATHER: *You are the Alpha and Omega and everything in between. Work in me as I work at being all You want me to be. I love everything about You, Lord, from A to Z! Amen.*

6
Giving a Lift
1 Tim. 2:1

God's Word tells us to pray for one another. If you don't have a prayer list, use this as a starter. Since this book is written for fathers (and those who love them), this partial prayer list will focus on our needs as brothers in Christ. Let's lift each other up in prayer.

Let us pray for fathers who are
- out of work and out of control.
- raising stepchildren.
- working on raising the level of integrity in their lives.
- feeling overburdened and need to unburden their concerns on the Lord.
- building a new home.
- struggling to build a savings account.
- striving to imitate Christ.
- experiencing no intimacy with their wives.

- coping with thoughts of divorce.
- having difficulty coping after divorce.
- experiencing physical pain.
- trying to keep from causing physical pain.
- grieving a loss.
- rejoicing at finding God's eternal promises of life.
- dealing with aging.
- dealing with aging parents.
- feeling lost.
- seeming to have lost compassionate feelings.
- honoring their wives and families and in turn are honoring God.
- growing in their faith.
- dying due to lack of faith.
- ministering to other families.
- traveling on business.
- busy traveling back to God's ways.
- not able to see their children.
- expecting a child.
- expecting other kinds of miracles.
- battling diseases or handicaps and all fathers battling the disease of sin.
- easily losing their patience.
- treating patients.

- learning to worship in Spirit and truth.
- having difficulty telling the truth.
- burdened by guilt.
- freed by God's forgiveness.
- behind prison walls.
- living in other kinds of prisons.
- putting work before God and family.
- working at putting God first.
- addicted to substances.
- working at a substantive friendship.
- dealing with the empty-nest syndrome.
- dealing with the empty-heart syndrome.
- rejoicing in their children's accomplishments.
- accomplishing the joyful task of teaching their children to rejoice in all circumstances.
- in the middle of a midlife crisis.
- in the middle of a midday prayer.
- putting their children through school.
- putting themselves through school.
- teenagers.
- with teenagers.
- working daily on making their marriage work.

- looking for help in making their marriage work.
- praying for others.
- strengthened by knowing others are praying for them.

FATHER TO FATHER: *Father, hear my prayers for other fathers. Send Your Holy Spirit to intercede with me for fathers throughout the world. In Jesus' name I pray. Amen.*

7
All I Need . . .
1 Cor. 2:2

Robert Fulghum wrote a charming personal credo a few years back that has become very popular, the best-seller *All I Really Need to Know I Learned in Kindergarten.* His thoughts were insightful, amusing, and delightful. Fulghum stated that all he really needed to know about how to live, what to do, and how to be—he learned in kindergarten.

It would be a great blessing if our children could one day write a similar credo titled "What I Really Need to Know I Learned from My Christian Father." With that title in mind, I will take poetic license and add a sequel to Fulghum's piece.

❈ ❈ ❈

Most of what I really needed to know about how to live, what to do, and how to be—I learned from my Christian father. I did not find wisdom at the top of the graduate school mountain, but in the sixth pew on the pulpit side, where each week I sat next to my father in church. Wisdom was also in the garage, where he taught me about creating birdhouses and values. Life wisdom was also found within my father's car, where we would share jokes and laughter, Bible stories, and other stories.

These are some things I learned (even if I didn't fully understand them at the time) from my Christian father: Share with others what God has shared with you. Respect others as you want to be respected. Give thanks. Play. Pray. Spend as much time praying as you do playing. Smile and laugh—a lot. Take 10 (commandments as a guide). Repent. Know God and His grace intimately. Rejoice! Forgive. It's OK (and good) to admit a wrong. Love the mom of the house. Have an attitude—patterned after that of Jesus. Live the Lord's Prayer.

When I go out without my father, I remember that my other Father is always with me. When I go out with them, I hold their hands tightly.

I recall the feeling lying in my father's arms at night, his aftershave scent, and the touch of his scratchy cheek against mine. I learned from that and hold that memory tightly too.

There were times on the ball field when the statistic book noted that I struck out. That wasn't the case in my father's book. He's a great coach, even from the bleachers.

My father read me devotions about Abraham, John, Paul, and Jesus. They all died. So will we someday. But we will join them—still living—thanks to the latter.

One story my father read me was from *the* Book about a cross and empty tomb that had the biggest word I had ever heard— *love!* Everything I need to know is somewhere in that word.

All I really need to know I learned from my father, because my father daily teaches me by living and sharing everything he knows about Jesus Christ.

❋ ❋ ❋

This would be a wonderful gift from our children. Earthly fathers are never perfect models, but they can see the reflection of the perfect model, Christ, in our lives.

The apostle Paul also had an important credo. Unfortunately, it isn't as well known or followed as Robert Fulghum's. It simply reads, "I resolved to know nothing while I was with you except Jesus Christ and him crucified" (1 Cor. 2:2). What a great credo for us to live as a gift for our children!

FATHER TO FATHER: *Teach me, Father, to model Your life as my children model mine. I resolve to know Christ crucified in my life and love. Through Christ I come to You. Amen.*

8
The Best Ever
1 Cor. 4:15

Children love bragging to other children about how their father is the biggest, best, or most talented. That was one childhood game in which I didn't participate, however.

But as I grew older, I found out many things about my father that I had never known—information that may have led to that childlike bragging if I had only been aware. I found out that my father was a very gifted and talented man. As I grew to know him, he became a favorite companion. We were friends who came to know a unique parent-child bond of friendship, trust, and caring, whether laughing and sharing jokes, getting down to business man to man, or even when we disagreed.

In my pursuit of getting to know this man, had I stumbled across the perfect father? By no means. But I had the tendency to close the shade on any imperfections he had, letting faultless characteristics shine through.

My youthful days had passed by the time I finally began to know my father and to appreciate him. In time I learned to love and respect my seemingly ageless dad. It was then, like a child, I could begin to brag that my father was the biggest, best, and most talented. He was the best there ever was!

He cared about what I cared about. He was attentive to my needs and concerns. He loved me and encouraged me. He was my dad! All this, yet we never attended a father-son banquet. All this, yet he never took the time to sign one of my report cards. All this and more, even though my father had died four months before I was born.

Most children have the opportunity to be raised with the love of one father. But through my father's death I found that God had blessed me with many "fathers."

I did not miss that parental figure during my childhood. I guess a person doesn't miss what he or she doesn't know. It was only after I began to search and question that the answers came: I had a father—in fact, I had many. He is the multifaceted, special friend and loving father in the people around me. When I need a father, he's there. He is any man who has taken the time to love me as a son, friend, or child of God.

Though I never had the opportunity to know my real father, I thank God that He has blessed me with many fathers to fill that role. Most significantly, I thank Him for the relationship He has created between us as perfect Father and less-than-perfect son!

I know I shouldn't brag, but it's difficult not to when you've got the biggest, best, and most talented Dad around, all rolled up in one. I'm grateful that God brought out His best in all of them and, in turn, has given me the best there ever was!

FATHER TO FATHER: *Heavenly Father, how grateful this son of Yours is for Your perfect love and example. Continue to raise up godly men in my life to reflect Your ways and affect the way I live, love, and learn. And make me a godly, fatherly example to others. In Jesus' name I pray. Amen.*

9
Bedside Thoughts
Ps. 121:2

It's nearing midnight. My children have been asleep for several hours now. After spending some quiet time sitting on their beds, I would like to share some of my random bedside thoughts.

- A few hours ago I prayed that the Lord and His angels would surround the three of you tonight. I wonder how many angels the Lord brought with Him. Is the room angel-packed as I sit in their midst on this holy ground?

- I wish I could put my ear to your head and listen to your dreams.

- You are growing so very fast. I remember when we put you in your first big bed with the railing. This big bed doesn't look so big anymore, but you do!

- I should have apologized for losing my patience with you today. You were just excited about doing something with me. You had spent the day in school and finally had a chance to run and shout. You have so much energy! I regret that I missed that time together. I will ask for your forgiveness tomorrow. I will ask God's forgiveness right now.

- Speaking of such energy, it's amazing to see your bodies so still after a day of running, talking, skipping rope, playing games, eating. Now your bodies rest. You need it. God didn't create you with bionic bodies. I have much to learn from you. The day is for work (and play in your case), and the night is for sleeping.

- When I tucked you in earlier, I said, "Sleep tight." I should have told you, "Sleep loose!" You'll have enough stress later in life that will cause sleep-tight nights. Sleep at peace.

- I really enjoyed our bedtime songfest. It was fun! I'm certain the angels we invited joined along as our background singers. I wonder if they can sing and smile at the same time?

- Your room is filled with memories: books and more books that have closed out many of your days, trophies, pictures, souvenirs . . . memories of days past. As you grow older, I wonder what you will remember and what things you won't recall that your mom and I hoped you would.

- These growing, resting bodies of yours are such miracles. It's amazing the things your brains are taking in for the very first time. You marvel at so much. To adults everything's old hat, and we miss the marvel. Keep reminding me to marvel.
- Benjamin, I love the gift of your imagination in which you saw an entire secret fort in the mountains. You created it out of blankets and boxes for your brother and sister, but your mom and I enjoyed it just as much.
- Sarah, thank you for the wonderful chalk pictures on the driveway that welcomed me home today. They were bright, creative, and fun. Tonight's rain will wash them away, but I'll keep a copy in my mental box of memories.
- Christopher, that giggle spree you went on during supper when Daddy did something silly made my week. Thank you!
- I love you—each of you—very, very much.
- *Dear guardian Lord, there is no need to*

close my eyes when I pray tonight, for I'm looking into Your eyes through these children. Thank You for sending the angels—the ones I can't see and the ones named Benjamin, Sarah, and Christopher. Keep them marveling at Your creation as they continue to teach me. Help me to love them as You love them. In Jesus' name I pray. Amen.

FATHER TO FATHER: *Father, as I reflect on the gift of my family, I see that they are reflections of Your grace. For that I am very grateful. In Your Son's name I pray. Amen.*